J/797.3

700250 Wakeboarding in the X Games

DATE DUE

1346	JAN 2 8 2005

BRODART, CO.   Cat. No. 23-221-003

700250

Blomquist, Christopher   J 797.3 Blo
Wakeboarding in the X Games

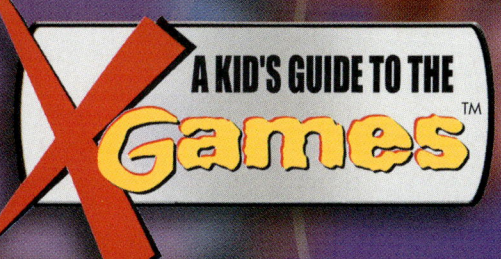

WAKEBOARDING

CHRISTOPHER BLOMQUIST

The Rosen Publishing Group's
PowerKids Press™
New York

For two Xtremely wonderful nephews, Timothy and James

**Safety gear, including buoyancy vests, helmets, and gloves, should be worn while wakeboarding.
Do not attempt tricks without proper gear, instruction, and supervision.**

Published in 2003 by The Rosen Publishing Group, Inc.
29 East 21st Street, New York, NY 10010

Copyright © 2003 by The Rosen Publishing Group, Inc.

All rights reserved. No part of this book may be reproduced in any form without permission in writing from the publisher, except by a reviewer.

First Edition.

Editor: Nancy MacDonell Smith
Book Design: Mike Donnellan and Michael de Guzman

Photo Credits: Cover, pp. 4, 7, 19, 21 © Icon Sports Media; p. 8 © Josh Letchworth; pp. 11, 12 © Mike Isler/Icon SMI; p. 15 © Patty Segovia/Icon SMI; p. 16 © Robert Beck/Icon SMI.

Blomquist, Christopher.
Wakeboarding in the X games / Christopher Blomquist.— 1st ed.
    p. cm. — (A kid's guide to the X Games)
Includes index.
  ISBN 0-8239-6301-2 (lib. bdg.)
1. Wakeboarding—Juvenile literature. 2. ESPN X-Games—Juvenile literature. [1. Wakeboarding. 2. ESPN X-Games.] I. Title.
GVx840.W34 B56 2003
797.3'2—dc21

2001007911

Manufactured in the United States of America

Contents

1	What Is Wakeboarding?	5
2	Wakeboarding at the X Games	6
3	Picking Boarders for the X Games	9
4	The First Wakeboarding Competitions	10
5	Some Great X-Games Moments	13
6	Star Wakeboarders at the X Games	14
7	The Wakeboarding Competition	17
8	The Wakeboarding Course	18
9	A Talk with Tara Hamilton	20
10	A Look Ahead	22
	Glossary	23
	Index	24
	Web Sites	24

Before competing at the 2001 X Games in Philadelphia, Pennsylvania, Danny Harf takes a practice run on the Schuylkill River.

What Is Wakeboarding?

In wakeboarding a person straps his or her feet to a board that floats in the water. A wakeboard is usually about 4 feet (122 cm) long and 1 foot (30.5 cm) wide. The rider then holds a rope that is attached to the back of a motorboat. When the boat moves, the rider is towed along.

The speeding boat forms a trail of waves, called a **wake**, behind it. A wakeboarder rides this wake and performs tricks on the board. Some of these tricks might be spins, twists, or **midair** flips.

When something is extreme, it is not common or everyday. Wakeboarding is not a common, well-known sport, such as basketball or football, so it is called an **extreme sport**. Extreme sports are also called action sports, because they are so exciting.

Wakeboarding at the X Games

The X Games is an event during which extreme sports are played. The X Games is held every summer and winter in the United States. Wakeboarding is part of the summer X Games.

At the X Games, **athletes** try to win prizes and money. Athletes who come in first win gold **medals**. Those who come in second win silver medals. Those who come in third win bronze medals.

Wakeboarding was not an X-Games sport until the second X Games in 1996. That year the men's wakeboarding event was **introduced**. The women's wakeboarding **competition** was added at the 1997 X Games.

Today X-Games wakeboarding events are very popular. About 7,000 people came to watch wakeboarding at the 2001 X Games in Philadelphia, Pennsylvania.

Some X Games fans are extremely devoted. Some of these fans even have fake tattoos that they wear while watching the competitions!

Before they can compete in the X Games, wakeboarders have to do well in other competitions.

Picking Boarders for the X Games

A company called World Sports and Marketing organizes the X Games wakeboarding events. It works with another group, the World Wakeboard Association (WWA), to choose judges and athletes. Most WWA members used to be, or still are, star wakeboarders.

An event called a **qualifier** is held a few months before the X Games. The five top-scoring men and the three top-scoring women from the qualifier get to compete at the X Games. The number of invited men is greater than the number of invited women because most of the world's wakeboarders are men.

The two gold medalists from the year before also return to the X Games. The gold medalist from the Asian X Games is invited, too. The top five men and the three best women from a competition called the Pro Wakeboard Tour also **qualify**.

The First Wakeboarding Competitions

The very first X Games was held in 1995 in Rhode Island. Those games were called the Extreme Games and did not have any wakeboarding events. In fact barefoot water jumping, which is like waterskiing without the skis, was the only water sport played. The next year, in 1996, two important changes were made. The competition's name was changed to the X Games. The other change was the inclusion of wakeboarding! That year the event was for men only. Fourteen-year-old Parks Bonifay of Florida won the very first X-Games wakeboarding gold medal. Jeremy Kovak, a 22-year-old from Ontario, Canada, won the silver. Scott Byerly, a 23-year-old American, won the bronze. In 1997, X-Games wakeboarding also became a women's event. Tara "Lil' Ripper" Hamilton, a 15-year-old from Florida, won the women's gold that year.

Parks Bonifay does a trick called an S-Bend at the 2001 X Games in Philadelphia. In this trick, a wakeboarder makes his or her body into the shape of an S in the air.

Darin Shapiro flips upside down on his board during one of his runs at the 2001 X Games.

Some Great X-Games Moments

At the 1999 X Games in San Francisco, California, Parks Bonifay won his second gold medal. The next year, Shane, Bonifay's younger brother, won the bronze.

In 2001, on the Schuylkill River in Philadelphia, two wakeboarding tricks were done that had never before been accomplished in a contest. First, 27-year-old Darin Shapiro of Florida did a **nine-hundred**, or two and one-half spins in the air. He did this trick off a ramp called a **kicker**. Then 20-year-old Erik Ruck of Wisconsin did a new and difficult **variation** of a **seven-hundred and twenty**, which is two full spins in the air. Later 16-year-old Danny Harf of Florida won the gold for a run that also featured a nine-hundred. Shapiro got the silver. Ruck won the bronze. The X-Games judges said the 2001 event was the best wakeboarding they had ever seen.

Star Wakeboarders at the X Games

Shapiro has wakeboarded in five X Games and has won a medal at each one. He won the gold medal in 1998 and in 2000. He won the silver medal in 1997, in 1999, and in 2001. No other wakeboarder has as many X-Games medals as Shapiro.

Hamilton is the most-decorated woman wakeboarder in X-Games history. She has four medals. She has one gold medal from the 1997 X Games, and one from the 2000 X Games, plus one bronze medal from the 1998 X Games and one from the 2001 X Games.

The newest young wakeboarding star is Dallas Friday of Orlando, Florida. In 2000, at the age of 13, she won the silver medal. In 2001, Friday won the gold! Friday used to be a gymnast, and she uses her gymnastic skills to shoot herself and the board high into the air.

Dallas Friday is only in her early teens, but she's already famous for her ability to handle a wakeboard.

 Professional wakeboarders sometimes don't wear safety equipment, but this sport can be dangerous, so it's smart to wear protective gear at all times.

The Wakeboarding Competition

In the men's wakeboarding competition at the X Games, the 16 invited athletes split into two groups of eight. In the first round, or **heat**, the men in the first group each do a run. For the second heat, the athletes in the second group each get a turn in the water. The best four from the first heat and the best four from the second heat then advance to the finals. In the finals, each athlete does another run. That run decides who wins the competition.

Just one round is needed to decide the winner in the women's wakeboarding event, because only eight athletes are invited to participate.

The Wakeboarding Course

The athletes use the floating **obstacles** placed in the course to do their amazing tricks. At the 2001 X Games, three obstacles were used.

The kicker is a short, steep ramp that can shoot riders 6 feet (2 m) into the air. Shapiro used it to do his nine-hundred.

The **slider** is a pipe that is 30 feet (9 m) long. The boarders can hop onto it with their boards and can slide along its smooth surface.

The third obstacle, called the **Slaughter Box**, looks like a big box. It floats about 3 feet (1 m) above the surface of the water in the middle of the course. Boarders can slide across it or can use its ramps to get themselves high into the air. Once they're in the air, they flip and spin.

Tara "Lil' Ripper" Hamilton sails past the Slaughter Box during the 2001 X Games in Philadelphia, Pennsylvania.

A Talk with Tara Hamilton

What does it feel like to participate in the X Games?
To participate in the X Games is **indescribable**. There are thousands of people watching, tons of cameras and reporters running around all over, and the nerves of all the athletes floating around in the air. It is one of my favorite contests.

How have the X Games changed over the years?
I think that the games are a lot more known by a lot more people.

What's your all-time favorite X-Games moment?
Winning the games [for a second time in 2000] has to be my best moment.

How do you personally prepare for an X-Games run?
I prepare for the games the same as any other contest and just practice hard and try not to get upset if I am riding bad the week

before (which I have the tendency to do).

What's ahead for wakeboarding and the X Games?
Wakeboarding seems to be growing more and more each year, so hopefully it will continue.

Any advice for kids who would like to try wakeboarding?
If you like the water then get out there and try wakeboarding. It is a fun sport and pretty easy to catch on to. Find someone with a boat or Jet Ski, go grab a wakeboard, and have a fun day out at the lake.

Tara Hamilton ▶

A Look Ahead

As wakeboarding becomes more popular in the world, the size of the X-Games crowds will continue to grow. X-Games wakeboarding in 2000 attracted a crowd of 4,500 people. Just a year later, 7,000 people came to see the sport's best stars compete.

The men's and women's wakeboarding events at the X Games will continue to bring the world's top riders together. Some of these riders will be new, young athletes like Dallas Friday. These kid stars will amaze the crowd and the judges with new tricks and probably will set new X-Games records.

More sliders will be added to the wakeboarding course at future X Games. Having more sliders will allow the athletes to do more tricks. This will make X-Games wakeboarding even more fun to watch. Believe it or not, future X-Games wakeboarding is going to be even wetter and wilder!

Glossary

athletes (ATH-leets) People who take part in sports.
competition (kom-peh-TIH-shun) A sports contest.
extreme sport (ek-STREEM SPORT) A sport such as wakeboarding, skateboarding, motocross, BMX, street luge, and in-line skating.
heat (HEET) A round in a race.
indescribable (ihn-dih-SKRY-buh-bul) Not being able to be talked about in words.
introduced (in-truh-DOOSD) Added or brought to.
kicker (KIH-kur) A short, steep ramp.
medals (MEH-dulz) Small, round pieces of metal that are given as awards.
midair (mid-AYR) Happening in the air.
nine-hundred (NYN HUN-dred) Two and one-half spins in the air.
obstacles (AHB-stih-kuhlz) Items put on the course to get in the boarders' way, such as ramps or pipes.
qualifier (KWAH-lih-fy-rer) A sports event held before the X Games to test which athletes will go to the X Games.
qualify (KWAH-lih-fy) To meet the requirements of something.
seven-hundred and twenty (SEH-ven HUN-dred AND TWEN-tee) Two full spins in the air.
Slaughter Box (SLAW-tur BOX) An obstacle on the course that looks like a big box.
slider (SLY-der) An obstacle on the course that is a long pipe.
variation (ver-ee-AY-shun) A different way of doing something.
wake (WAYK) The wavy trail a boat leaves behind itself as it moves through the water.

Index

A
Asian X Games, 9

B
boat, 5, 21
Bonifay, Parks, 10, 13

F
Friday, Dallas, 14, 22

H
Hamilton, Tara "Lil' Ripper," 10, 14, 20–21
Harf, Danny, 13
heat, 17

K
Kovak, Jeremy, 10

M
medal(s), 6, 10, 13–14

N
nine-hundred, 13

P
Philadelphia, Pennsylvania, 6, 13
Pro Wakeboard Tour, 9

Q
qualifier, 9

R
Ruck, Erik, 13

S
Schuylkill River, 13
seven-hundred and twenty, 13
Shapiro, Darin, 13–14, 18
Slaughter Box, 18
slider(s), 18, 22

W
wake, 5
World Sports and Marketing, 9
World Wakeboard Association (WWA), 9

Web Sites

Due to the changing nature of Internet links, PowerKids Press has developed an online list of Web sites related to the subject of this book. This site is updated regularly. Please use this link to access the list: www.powerkidslinks.com/kgxg/wakeinx/